African Americans
IN MINNESOTA

Nora Murphy and Mary Murphy-Gnatz

TELLING OUR OWN STORIES

 MINNESOTA HISTORICAL SOCIETY PRESS

Minnesota Historical Society Press
St. Paul

Printed in Canada

♾ The paper used in this publication meets the minimum requirements of the American National Standard for Information Sciences—Permanence for Printed Library Materials, ANSI Z39.48-1984.

Denise Kalschuer, Reading Specialist
Alvin Carter, Original Drawings
Cartography, Carto-Graphics
Christine Thillen, Copy Editor
Peregrine Graphic Services, Composition

Credits: Drawing pp. 6, 8, Alvin Carter; Photo p. 10, Courtesy of James Griffin; *Weekly Trumpet* p. 10, Courtesy of David Taylor; Photo p. 11, Rebecca Dallinger; Drawing pp. 12, 13, Alvin Carter; Photo p. 17, National Archives of Canada and National Library of Canada; Excerpt p. 18, *Collections of the State Historical Society of Wisconsin*, vol. 18, 1908; Photo p. 24, Courtesy of David Taylor; Drawing pp. 25, 28, Alvin Carter; Article p. 31, *Northwestern Bulletin Appeal*; Photo p. 32, Courtesy of David Taylor; Drawing p. 33, Alvin Carter; Photo and Caption p. 40, *The Appeal*; Drawing pp. 42, 45, Alvin Carter; Headline p. 47, *Star Tribune*; Drawing p. 56, Alvin Carter; Photos pp. 52, 53, 54, 55, 58, 59, 61, Courtesy of James Griffin; Drawing p. 62, Alvin Carter; Photo p. 63, Courtesy of David Taylor; Article p. 70, Courtesy of David Taylor; Photo p. 71, Courtesy of David Taylor; Drawing p. 71, Alvin Carter; Photos pp. 72, 73, 75, 78, 79, 80, 81, Rebecca Dallinger; Photo on left, p. 77, Courtesy of Alvin Carter.

All other photos and documents, courtesy of the Minnesota Historical Society.

Staff Credits: Maureen Otwell, Assistant Director for Museums; Carol Schreider, Head of Education; Sara Schroeder Yaeger, Education Publications Manager; Nora Murphy, Curriculum Writer; Jennifer Goldman, Teacher Education Specialist; Mary Murphy-Gnatz, Research Assistant; Dominic Abram, Researcher.

African Americans in Minnesota: Telling Our Own Stories was made possible in part through the generous financial support of Whitney and Elizabeth MacMillan.

Library of Congress Cataloging-in-Publication Data

Murphy, Nora.
   African Americans in Minnesota : telling our own stories / by Nora Murphy and Mary Murphy-Gnatz.
      p. cm.
   Includes bibliographical references and index.
   Summary: Stories of the lives and times of nine African-American children and adults whose contributions to Minnesota's history span nearly two centuries, from the early 1800s to the present day.
   ISBN 0-87351-380-0 (pbk. : alk. paper)
   1. Afro-Americans—Minnesota—Biography—
      Anecdotes—Juvenile literature.
   2. Afro-Americans—Minnesota—History—
      Anecdotes—Juvenile literature.
   3. Minnesota—Biography—Anecdotes—Juvenile
      literature. [1. Minnesota—History. 2. Afro-
      Americans—Biography.] I. Murphy-Gnatz, Mary.
   II. Title.

F615.N4 M87 2000
977.6'00496073'00922—dc21
                                                      99-054539

Contents

Storytelling and History

Imagine it's a cool morning and you are standing outside with your friend, waiting for the bus. You notice your friend is wearing a new hat. The hat is made from colorful cloth. "Hey, where did you get that hat?" you ask. Your friend tells you a story about the hat. Turns out, it was made from West African cloth but not in Africa. Your friend's aunt made the hat right here in Minnesota.

The bus finally arrives, and you take a seat next to the window. As you gaze out the window, you start thinking about the man who came to talk to your class yesterday. The man was a **historian** named Dr. David Taylor. Dr. Taylor said, "History is a collection of stories." Even stories like the story of your friend's new hat? Why not!

Your friend's story about the hat gets you thinking more about African Americans in Minnesota. When did Africans first come to Minnesota? What did they do when they got here? You don't know the answers yet, but you do know where to find them. If you want to know more about the history of African Americans in Minnesota, you have to find stories about blacks in Minnesota's past. But first, you need to start at the beginning. You need to know a little bit about Africa itself.

Life in Africa

Africa is a **continent** that is larger than all of North America and three times bigger than the United States. Many scientists believe that Africa was the birthplace of human life. Some of the first Africans lived in the upper half of the continent. After thousands of

Objects can tell us stories from history, too. This hat looks like a West African hat, but it was made in the United States in the 1990s. It is kept at the Minnesota History Center in St. Paul to help tell the history of African Americans in Minnesota.

years, the land there grew very dry. The people had to move to different parts of Africa. As they moved, Africans formed different types of communities, kingdoms, and cities all over the continent.

Life in the African cities was more like life in an American city than you might realize. People lived busy lives, working at many different kinds of jobs. There were doctors and cooks, teachers and soldiers, shopkeepers and historians.

When Europeans (*YER-uh-PEE-ins*) and other outsiders first arrived in Africa, they discovered that parts of Africa were very rich in rubber, oils, gold, and diamonds. The Europeans began trading with the Africans for these things.

In Africa, as in most of the world at that time, some people were slaves. They were owned by other people and forced to work. But in Africa, many slaves were able to become part of the family and community.

Later, Europeans and Africans traded for African slaves to work in North and South America. African slaves were captured by force and sent in ships to the Americas.

Historians in West Africa

Historians in West Africa are called **griots** (*GREE-ohs*). They learned by listening to stories about people and things that happened in the past. Then the griots told these stories to their own students.

A West African griot passed down this story about a boy named Sundjata (*Soon-JAH-tah*). Sundjata became a king in the 1200s. He lived in Mali (*MAH-lee*). Mali is in West Africa, which is where many **ancestors** of present-day African Americans lived.

Several years before Sundjata was born, a wise woman told the king of Mali that he would have a son. This son

King Sundjata ruled the kingdom of Mali hundreds of years ago. This map shows Mali in West Africa in the 1990s.

"Using all his strength, the boy pulled with both hands and stood up. The iron rod bent under his new strength!"

Sundjata because he could not run and play or do other things boys his age could do. But his father never gave up on him. He knew his son would grow up and become king. To prepare him to be king, Sundjata's father asked the griot Balla Fasseke (*Fa-SAY-kay*) to teach Sundjata about the history of Mali.

When he was seven years old, Sundjata decided he would learn to walk. He asked the village blacksmith to make him an iron rod. The blacksmith had been saving a huge rod for a special occasion. This special iron rod was so heavy that six men were needed to carry it. When the men placed the rod in front of him, Sundjata lifted it up with just one hand. Using all his strength, the boy pulled with both hands and stood up. The iron rod bent under his new strength! After that, Sundjata walked like all the other children in the village.

would become the mightiest king ever to rule in West Africa. The woman also said the boy's mother would have a crooked back and big eyes. The king did indeed marry a woman like that. She gave birth to their son Sundjata in the year 1217.

As a young child, Sundjata could not use his legs. He crawled on all fours and did not walk. Everyone laughed at

Sundjata the Student and Ruler

After he learned to walk, Sundjata continued his studies. The griot Fasseke wasn't his only teacher. His mother told Sundjata and his friends stories about the plants and the animals in the forests. Older men in the village taught Sundjata how to hunt. Later he studied the art of war with a king in East Africa.

When Sundjata returned to Mali, enemies were trying to take over his country. Sundjata used all the skills he had learned from his many teachers. He defeated his enemies and made the Kingdom of Mali bigger than ever before. Under King Sundjata, Mali became one of the most peaceful and richest kingdoms in West Africa.

Exploring the Americas

After King Sundjata died, his family continued to rule in Mali, including Abu Bakr (*AH-boo Bah-KAR*). King Abu Bakr was a very curious person. He wanted to know what was on the other side of the Atlantic Ocean. He sent thousands of boats from Africa to explore. His ships discovered special currents in the ocean. Currents are like fast-moving rivers. A ship sailing on this river in the ocean moves faster and easier. The currents Abu Bakr's ships found led the explorers west to the Americas. Later, European slave traders used these same currents to carry African slaves to North and South America. Some historians believe that King Abu Bakr's ships landed in America long before the slave trade.

Pedro Alonza Niña (*PAY-dro Ah-LON-za NEEN-yah*) was another famous African explorer. He guided a ship from Europe to the Americas for Christopher Columbus more than 500 years ago.

African American Stories in Minnesota

Now that you have heard a few stories about Africa and about Africans who explored the Americas, it's time to move on to Minnesota. King Sundjata and King Abu Bakr didn't come to Minnesota, of course, but other Africans did. African Americans have lived and worked in Minnesota for more than 200 years. They have all contributed to the Minnesota you know today.

George Bonga was the first African American born in Minnesota. He grew up in what is now northern Minnesota. As a young boy, he learned how to **canoe** on the many lakes and rivers in our state. George learned how to hunt and fish. He spoke three languages. He grew up to be a famous fur trader. He also helped the United States government buy lands from the Ojibwe (*Oh-JIB-way*) that are part of Minnesota today. To learn more about him,

George Bonga was a fur trader and interpreter for American Indians and the United States government.

Robert Hickman, John's father, led 76 slaves to freedom in Minnesota on a raft like this one.

read the story "Meet George Bonga" on page 12.

William Grey and **John Hickman** both moved to Minnesota 150 years ago. But they didn't come here the same way. William and his family took a train and a **steamboat**. John and his family came by raft up the Mississippi River. William and John and their families helped make a better life for African

Sawmills lined the Mississippi River in Minneapolis when Mattie McIntosh was growing up in the 1880s.

Americans in our state. If you want to learn what they did, read the story "Meet William Grey and John Hickman" on page 22.

The McIntosh (*MAC-in-tosh*) family lived and worked near the Mississippi River in Minneapolis more than 100 years ago. Their second-youngest daughter was named **Mattie McIntosh**. Her mother worked at Fort Snelling. Mrs. McIntosh rode a **horse trolley** to get to work at the fort. Mattie's father worked in a sawmill near their house in Minneapolis. In fact, Mr. McIntosh could walk to work. To find out more about Mattie's life and what she studied at school, read "Meet Mattie McIntosh" on page 32.

Nellie Stone Johnson grew up on a farm in central Minnesota in the early 1900s. One of her favorite things to do as a kid was to ride her horse. She rode her horse to deliver newspapers to the farmers. Her family also owned one of the earliest cars—a Model T Ford. When she grew up, Nellie helped make new laws to help Minnesotans, especially African Americans and women. If you want to know what kinds of laws she worked on, read the story "Meet Nellie Stone Johnson" on page 42.

James Griffin grew up in St. Paul, the capital city of Minnesota. His father worked on the railroad and traveled all

Nellie Stone Johnson, upper right, was the oldest child in her family. She was about 10 years old when this photo was taken.

James Griffin, shown here early in his career, served in the St. Paul Police Department for more than 40 years.

around the country. James liked to play sports when he was young. He was very good at basketball and football. When he grew up, James tried working on the railroad like his father, but he didn't like it. He tried playing basketball on a semi-pro team, but it didn't pay well. Finally, he decided to become a police officer. If you read the story "Meet James Griffin" on page 52, you can find out how he became the deputy chief in St. Paul.

David Taylor also grew up in St. Paul. David also liked sports, but he liked reading even more. He and his friends liked to write stories. For two years, they wrote and sold a community newspaper. The boys walked all over the neighborhood to gather information for their newspaper. When David had to go downtown, he usually rode a **streetcar**. When he grew up he became a historian, or a modern griot. If you want to hear a story from David's past—like the time his pushcart almost caught on fire—read "Meet David Taylor" on page 62.

David Taylor and his friends wrote and published this newspaper, the Weekly Trumpet, *when they were in elementary school.*

In 1996 **Eric Mosley** and his family moved to St. Paul from Chicago. That same year, **Mahamoud Aden Amin** (*Ma-HA-mood AH-deen AH-meen*) and his family flew to Minneapolis from Mogadishu, Somalia (*Mo-ga-DEE-shoo, So-MAH-lee-ya*). Eric and Mahamoud have many things in common. But there are also many differences between them. For example, Africa is the homeland for both boys and their families. But Eric's ancestors probably left Africa by force hundreds of years ago. Mahamoud's family chose to leave Africa. To find out why their families left Africa, read the story "Meet Eric Mosley and Mahamoud Aden Amin" on page 72.

Becoming a Griot

The school day is over, and you're heading back home. Your backpack is stuffed with seven stories that will tell you more about George Bonga, William Grey, John Hickman, Mattie McIntosh, Nellie Stone Johnson, James Griffin, David Taylor, Eric Mosley, and Mahamoud Aden Amin. After you have read them, you can be a griot, ready to share many stories of African Americans in Minnesota.

Mahamoud Aden Amin was born in Somalia, a country in East Africa.

Eric Mosley and Mahamoud Aden Amin met while making sweet potato pie at the Minnesota History Center in St. Paul.

Meet George Bonga

Ojibwe hunters traded beaver pelts for trade goods such as this metal kettle. Kettles were used for cooking and carrying water.

Imagine you've fallen asleep and you're dreaming. It's winter in northern Minnesota, and you are standing under a pine tree that is covered in snow. In front of you is a long, narrow building made of logs. The building drips with melting ice. You wonder what's inside, so you step forward and peek through a crack between logs. People fill the room inside. Who are they? What are they doing? You decide to go inside and find out.

Once the door opens, you see a group of American Indian men standing in front of a long, low wooden counter. The counter is filled with some tin kettles, a gun, and two wool blankets with stripes. The American Indian men are looking at the **trade goods** very carefully. Is this some kind of store, you wonder?

No one notices you as you step up to the long counter to see better. A tall African American man is standing behind the counter. You get the feeling this man is selling the kettles, the gun, and the blankets. He is talking to the American Indian men. You can't understand them because no one is speaking English. They are all speaking Ojibwe (*Oh-JIB-way*), the language of the American Indian tribe in northern Minnesota.

After a while, the Ojibwe men turn around and walk to the front of the room where they have left their stack of beaver **pelts**—stretched, cleaned beaver skins with the fur still on them. One by one, the men count their pelts and walk back to the counter. They give their pelts to the man behind the counter. In return, he gives them some kettles, a gun, and some blankets. Then the Ojib-we men say good-bye to the trader and leave the log building with their new things.

The room is quiet now, except for the sound of the African American man cleaning the counter and stacking the pelts. He turns around, gives you a big smile, and says, "Welcome to my trading post! I'm George Bonga. What do you have to trade today?" You realize you don't have anything to trade—and then you wake up. You are curious to find out more about traders like George Bonga, who lived in Minnesota 200 years ago.

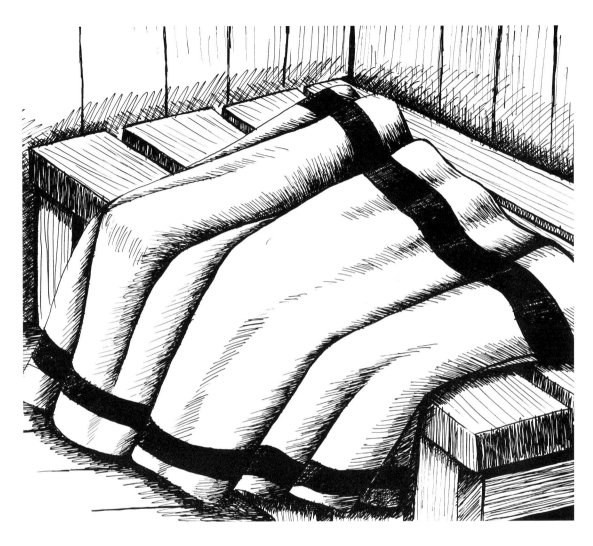

Guns and blankets like the ones shown here were popular items for trade when George Bonga was a fur trader.

The Fur Trade: Minnesota's First Big Business

George Bonga was a fur trader and interpreter in Minnesota. He spoke three languages: English, French, and Ojibwe.

When George Bonga was growing up, Minnesota wasn't a state yet. The land looked very different, too. Trees covered much of the area. The only roads were walking trails on land and canoe **routes** along our lakes, rivers, and streams. American Indians had used these paths for thousands of years to trade all across North America.

In the late 1600s and 1700s, explorers from other continents traveled to the middle of North America. These explorers were looking for animals with fur. They could sell the furs in Europe (*YER-up*) and make a lot of money. The most popular of all the fur animals was the beaver. Europeans (*YER-uh-PEE-ins*) loved wearing beaver hats because they looked fancy and were **waterproof**.

Europeans bought beaver pelts from North America and made them into fashionable hats.

The explorers found woods and lakes that were home to many different animals, such as beaver, muskrat, raccoon, deer, and bear. Soon the fur trade grew. It was a big business in Minnesota for 200 years.

Three groups worked in the fur trade in Minnesota: fur traders, American Indian hunters, and canoers— or **voyageurs** (*voy-ah-JERS*). The hunters brought the animal pelts to the fur traders. In return, the fur traders gave the hunters European-made trade goods such as blankets, kettles, and guns. Then the traders hired voyageurs to load the pelts onto their long canoes and paddle them to big ships headed for Europe.

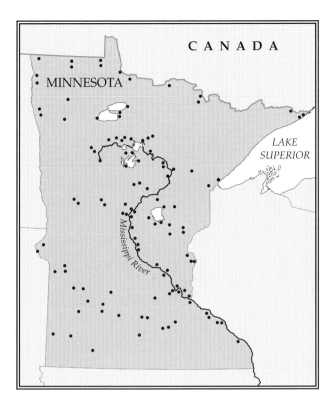

The fur trade was Minnesota's first big business. This map shows many of the fur posts in the area through 1850.

The Bongas: An Early African American Family in Minnesota

George Bonga was the first African American born in Minnesota. He was born in 1802 near Lake Superior and what is now the city we call Duluth. He and his family were fur traders.

George Bonga's grandfather Jean Bonga arrived in this part of the country in the 1700s. He worked at an English trading post and fort in what is now Michigan. When Jean first came to the trading post, he was a **slave**. A slave is a person who is owned by another person. Slaves do not get paid for their work. They must do what their owner says.

This 1827 drawing by Thomas L. McKenney shows what a fur post near Duluth looked like. George Bonga may have lived here.

Harriet and Dred Scott were slaves who met and married at Fort Snelling. When they left Minnesota, they went to court to fight for their freedom.

Slavery has never been legal in Minnesota. But when George Bonga was alive, some European and American army officers brought slaves to work in Minnesota from the South, where slavery was still legal. For example, Harriet and Dred Scott were two slaves who were brought to work at Fort Snelling, near St. Paul. They met, married, and worked at the fort. Later, the Scotts and their owners left Minnesota. The Scotts believed they should be free because they had lived in a free state. They went to the U.S. Supreme Court. The Supreme Court makes decisions about laws for everyone in the country. But the court ruled against the Scotts and denied them their freedom.

Jean Bonga did not have to go to court to seek freedom. His owner gave him his freedom in Michigan. Jean married a black woman named Marie

George's grandparents Jean and Marie Jeanne Bonga were legally married in 1794. Notice the spelling differences in their names. In the French language Jean is a male name, and Jeanne is a female name.

June 25, 1794, I, the undersigned priest and apostolic Missionary, Received the mutual consent of jean Bouga and of jeanne, the former a negro and the latter a negress, both free, and I gave them the nuptial Benediction in the presence of the following witnesses, towit: Messr. jean Nicolas Marchesseaux, hamelin, the elder, francois Soulignny, charles chandonnet, some of whom signed; the others, being unable to write, made their usual marks. * * *

Le Dru, apostolic Missionary.[32]

Jeanne at the trading post. Jean and Marie Bonga's son Pierre became a respected fur trader in Minnesota. Later Pierre Bonga married an Ojibwe woman there. She gave birth to their son George in 1802.

Like other fur trader families, the Bongas probably lived in a simple log home, heated with a fireplace. When he was a child, George Bonga may have worn a mix of Ojibwe and European clothes. He learned how to hunt like the Ojibwe hunters and how to canoe like the voyageurs. When he grew older, George Bonga went to school in Montreal (*MON-tree-ALL*), Canada. When he returned to Minnesota, he worked in the fur trade like his father and his grandfather.

George Bonga in the Fur Trade

George Bonga began his work in the fur trade by taking pelts and trade goods across the lakes and rivers of Minnesota. He was famous for his strength. People who knew him wrote that he was over six feet tall and weighed more than 200 pounds. They also reported that he could carry 700 pounds of furs and supplies all at once!

Voyageurs carried animal pelts across lakes and rivers by canoe. The voyageurs in this painting by Frances Anne Hopkins are waking up on a foggy morning.

The voyageurs worked very hard for little pay. They also had only a few kinds of food. They traded with the Ojibwe for dried meat and wild rice. They also ate lots of pea soup. Here's one visitor's description of how voyageurs made breakfast overnight:

The tin kettle, in which they cooked their food, would hold eight or ten gallons. It was hung over the fire, nearly full of water, then nine quarts of peas—one quart per man, the daily allowance—were put in; and when they were well bursted, two or three pounds of pork, cut into strips, for seasoning, were added and allowed to boil or simmer till daylight. . . . [The soup was] so thick that a stick would stand upright in it.

Many voyageurs sang while they canoed. George Bonga sang, too. One man wrote that he "got up an excursion on the lake in a splendid birchbark canoe, manned by twelve men who paddled to the music of a French-Canadian boat song, led by himself."

George's Bonga's brother Stephen was an interpreter, too. He signed an 1837 treaty between the Ojibwe and the United States government.

George Bonga's signature is on an 1867 treaty signed between the Ojibwe and the United States government.

Later, George Bonga became a fur trader like his father. He worked with the American Fur Company at trading posts around the state. George traded pelts and goods with the Ojibwe.

George Bonga the Interpreter

George Bonga learned many important skills as a child and as a fur trader. He knew the land and the waterways of Minnesota. He knew many Ojibwe people. He also spoke both Ojibwe and English. George Bonga used these skills to help the U.S. government buy land from the Indian people.

He first helped the United States buy lands from the Ojibwe when he was only 18 years old. The U.S. government men spoke only English, and many of the Ojibwe spoke only Ojibwe. George Bonga was the **interpreter**. Since he spoke both languages, he helped the

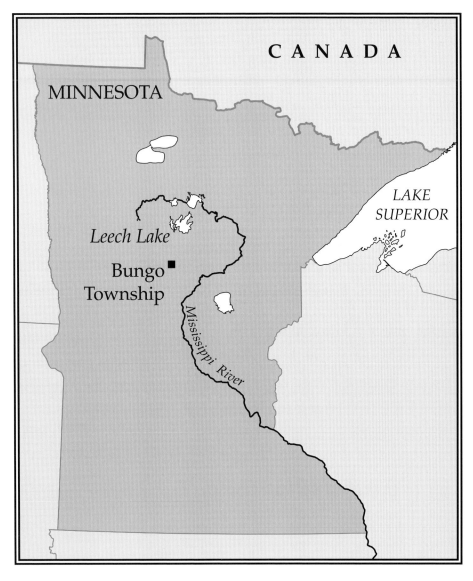

Late in his life, George Bonga settled near Leech Lake. Bungo Township in Cass County was named after the Bonga family, even though the spelling is different.

two groups talk to each other and sign **treaties**.

In 1837 his brother Stephen Bonga was an interpreter when the Ojibwe and the U.S. government signed a treaty at Fort Snelling. In this treaty, the Ojibwe gave up much of their land in central Minnesota and moved to other parts of the area. Thirty years later, George Bonga helped the U.S. government and the Ojibwe sign an 1867 treaty.

George Bonga and His Many Friends

When he was almost 40 years old, George Bonga married an Ojibwe woman named Ashwinn from Leech Lake in north-central Minnesota. They had four children: James, Peter, William, and Suzan. George taught his sons how to work in the fur trade, too. But by the time James, Peter, and

William were old enough to become traders, the beaver was almost extinct, and beaver hats were no longer popular in Europe.

When George was an older man, he and Ashwinn ran a lodge, a place where travelers could stay, rest, and eat. One traveler wrote that Mrs. Bonga cooked the best fish he'd ever eaten!

George Bonga was an important trader in Minnesota's earliest business, the fur trade. He helped the Ojibwe and the U.S. government work together to sell and buy the land that is now Minnesota. When he died, he left many friends all across the state. Governors, hunters, judges, traders, American Indians, and newcomers to Minnesota all counted the tall, strong George Bonga as their friend.

George Bonga's son William began working in the fur trade with his father but later became a farmer.

Meet William Grey and John Hickman

William Grey moved to Minnesota in 1857, and John Hickman came in 1863. William's family came from Pennsylvania to start a business. John's family escaped from slavery in Missouri.

This is a story about two boys who moved to Minnesota 150 years ago. William Grey and his family left home to start a new business in Minnesota. William came by train all across the eastern half of the United States. John Hickman and his family left home to escape **slavery**. John got to Minnesota on a **raft** that slowly made its way north up the Mississippi River.

William and John didn't know each other, and they didn't come to Minnesota for the same reasons. But they did have many things in common. They were both African Americans. Both of their families worked hard to build a safe and happy **community** in Minnesota. And both William and John contributed their skills to our state.

African Americans and Slavery in the United States

Before you can understand the differences and the similarities between the lives of William and John, you need to know about the history of slavery in the United States.

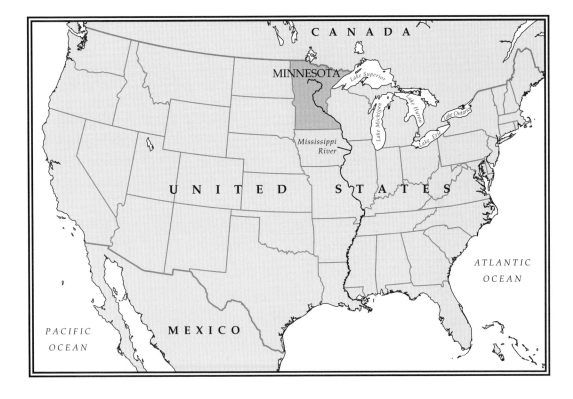

CANADA

MINNESOTA

Lake Superior

Lake Michigan

Lake Huron

Lake Ontario

Lake Erie

Mississippi River

UNITED STATES

ATLANTIC OCEAN

MEXICO

PACIFIC OCEAN

Starting about 400 years ago, millions of Africans were taken from their homes in West and Central Africa and sold to slaveowners in the Caribbean (*KARE-uh-BEE-un*) Islands, South America, and North America. In the United States, African slaves worked mainly in the southern part of the country, growing crops such as cotton, sugar, and tobacco. Enslaved Africans were not paid for their work.

By 1810, most blacks in the northern United States were free. Some slaves in the South and free blacks in the North began working with whites to end slavery. These people were called **abolitionists**. Abolitionist Frederick Douglass wrote about his childhood as a slave:

I suffered much from hunger, but much more from cold. In the hottest summer and coldest winter, I was kept almost naked—no shoes, no stockings, no jacket, no trousers, nothing on but a . . . shirt, reaching to my knees. I had no bed. . . . I used to steal a bag and sleep on the cold, damp, clay floor, with my head in and my feet out. My feet have been so cracked with the frost, that the pen with which I am writing might be laid in the gashes.

Americans disagreed over slavery. Many in the North did not support slavery, especially the spread of slavery into the West. The South did. Southerners wanted to use slave labor to develop the land in the West. Abraham Lincoln was elected president in 1860 after promising slavery would not be allowed

Frederick Douglass

More than 200,000 African Americans like this young soldier fought in the Civil War, including 104 African Americans from Minnesota.

to spread outside the South if he were president. The southern states were angry, and left the United States of America to form a new country, called the Confederate States of America. Lincoln wanted to keep the country together, so a war between the states broke out. It became known as the Civil War.

In 1863, during the war, President Lincoln issued the Emancipation Proclamation. This made it clear that if the North won the war, all slaves would be free. In 1865 the North did win the Civil War, and U.S. lawmakers passed the Thirteenth Amendment to the Constitution that made slavery illegal all across the country.

Growing up before the Civil War

William Grey and John Hickman were both born in the 1850s, before the Civil War started. William was born in Pennsylvania, where slavery was against the law. John was born in Missouri, where most African American families like his were slaves.

Being born in a free state meant that the Grey family had more opportunities than the Hickman family did. The Greys were business owners. The Hickmans were slaves. The Greys earned and saved money. The Hickmans probably never got money for their work as slaves. As a child in Pennsylvania, William could go to school. When he was a child in Missouri, it was against the law for John to go to school or learn to read.

But both families decided to move to Minnesota. The Greys were looking for ways to make more money. The Hickmans were looking for freedom. Minnesota offered both.

William Grey Travels to Minnesota

William's father, Ralph Grey, was a barber. Mr. Grey moved to Minnesota in

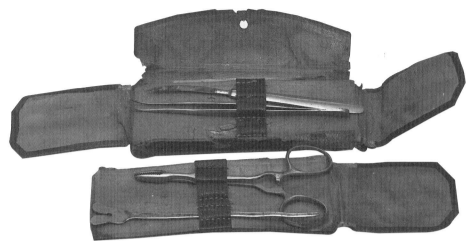

Barbers in the 1850s like Ralph Grey used kits like this one.

William and his mother rode in a stagecoach like the one below.

1855 to join his brother and start a new **barbershop** in the town of St. Anthony, which is now a part of Minneapolis. When William was two, he and his mother, Emily, joined his father in Minnesota.

People traveled to Minnesota in the late 1850s in several different ways. Some rode in wagons pulled by horses or oxen. People with more money took trains and steamboats. The Greys rode a train from Pennsylvania to Prairie

The Greys made a new home in the town of St. Anthony, pictured above. St. Anthony became a part of Minneapolis in 1872.

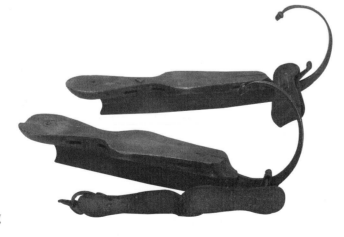

Children growing up in Minnesota in the 1860s used skates for fun during the winter.

du Chien, Wisconsin, where the railroad line ended. Mrs. Grey wrote about the food along the way:

> It was ham and eggs for breakfast, eggs and ham for dinner, and . . . for supper we were given the same old dish—ham and eggs!

After the Greys reached Prairie du Chien, they took a steamboat up the Mississippi River to St. Paul. From there, they rode in a **stagecoach** to St. Anthony for one dollar. We don't have stagecoaches anymore, but it still costs about a dollar to ride the city bus from St. Paul to Minneapolis!

Growing up in St. Anthony

Mr. Grey earned good money as a barber. The Greys could live well in Minnesota. When William and his mother arrived in St. Anthony, the Grey family bought an old barn that had been turned into a house. Mrs. Grey put pretty wallpaper on the walls and bought new furniture. She paid eight dollars for a rocking chair and one dollar each for some plain chairs.

In Pennsylvania, Mrs. Grey had served her family fresh fruits and vegetables. She had to learn new ways of cooking in Minnesota because there wasn't much fresh food available. Neighbors taught her how to make pork and beans, sauerkraut (*SOW-er-krowt*), pickled pig, and Irish potatoes.

William had a sister and a brother who were both born in Minnesota. In fact, his little brother was the first African American born in either St. Anthony or Minneapolis. The Grey children probably went to school in St. Anthony. After school, William may have helped his father at his new barbershop in a hotel near the Mississippi River.

Growing up in St. Anthony, William must have learned a lot about slavery and the abolition movement. Mrs. Grey and her parents were abolitionists back in Pennsylvania. In Minnesota, the Greys continued to work to end slavery. When abolitionist Frederick Douglass came to Minnesota for a visit, he stayed at the Greys' home.

Mrs. Grey, with the help of the minister at her church, helped a woman named Eliza Winston escape slavery. She was brought to Minnesota by a Southern slave owner in 1860. One night the police came to the Greys' house looking for Eliza Winston. She was hiding there, but the police didn't find her. Later, Eliza Winston won her freedom.

John Hickman Travels to Minnesota

John's father Robert Hickman was a **minister**. After learning about the Emancipation Proclamation, Mr. Hickman helped his family and 76 other slaves make the dangerous trip to find freedom in Minnesota. They called themselves Pilgrims.

Families lit their homes with candle lanterns in the 1860s.

John was only five when they left Missouri.

The Pilgrims did not have money or the freedom to buy tickets for a train or a steamboat. They had to travel on a handmade raft up the Mississippi River. Traveling that way isn't easy. Rafts don't have roofs or kitchens or beds. When it rains, you get wet. When it's time to eat, there's no place to cook food. When it's time to sleep, you have to lie down on the wood floor.

Robert Hickman, John's father, was well known for his bravery and leadership.

Robert Hickman and his followers used a wooden raft to make their dangerous escape up the Mississippi River to Minnesota in 1863.

But getting wet, hungry, and tired were small problems for the Pilgrims. Slave catchers watched the river carefully, looking for people like the Pilgrims trying to escape to the North. If they got caught, the slaves were brought back to their owners and beaten. Sometimes family members were separated and sold to new owners.

St. Paul in the late 1850s was a much smaller city than it is today.

The Pilgrims had to be very careful not to run into any slave catchers as they journeyed up the Mississippi River. They probably poled the raft at night and hid along the shore during the day. Luckily, the Pilgrims met a large steamboat called the *Northerner* on the river. The *Northerner* protected them and pulled the raft much of the way to St. Paul.

Their troubles didn't end in Minnesota. When the Pilgrims reached St. Paul, they were met by a group of angry Irish workers. These workers were afraid the Pilgrims would take their jobs. They didn't let the raft stop in St. Paul. The Pilgrims had no choice but to travel farther up the river to Fort Snelling. Later, many of the Pilgrims moved to St. Paul.

Growing up in St. Paul

John and the Hickman family settled in St. Paul. Mr. Hickman started one of the first African American churches in the state. He named it Pilgrim Baptist Church. It is still an active church today.

Pilgrim Baptist Church in St. Paul was founded by Robert Hickman and is still active today. In 1928 church members celebrated their new building.

Minnesota students like William and John probably practiced writing on slates like this one.

For more than 100 years, Pilgrim Baptist Church has been an important center for African Americans in St. Paul. For example, African American men could not vote in Minnesota when John first arrived here. John's father and other men in the community wanted to change that. The men met at Pilgrim Baptist Church to work on a plan. Their plan worked. In 1868, when John was 10, African American men finally got the right to vote in Minnesota. More than 50 years would pass before women would get the right to vote in the United States.

When John was growing up, he was a part of the Pilgrim Baptist Church, too. He went to Sunday School there. But that wasn't the only school John attended in St. Paul. He went to a one-room schoolhouse called Miss Bray's School, which was downtown on West Seventh Street.

The Civil War ended in 1865, when John was seven. Many Minnesotans, including more than 100 African Americans, served in the war. John told his own children about celebrating the end of the Civil War in St. Paul. John's son wrote in a newspaper article about his father's memories of the neighborhood celebration:

> Bonfires [and] booming guns proclaimed the event. Third Street, our "main street" was decorated and at night candles were burned in the store windows and in the windows of many private dwellings.

William and John Go to Work

There were not many job choices for African Americans when William and John started working as teenagers. But by the time they were grown-ups, both men had excellent jobs.

William Grey began working for the Chicago, Milwaukee, and St. Paul Railroad. Later, William joined the Railway

As chief clerk, William Grey was in charge of workers in a railway mail car like this one.

Mail Service and earned very good pay as a chief clerk. When he wasn't working, he enjoyed singing, dancing, and going to the theater.

John Hickman started delivering packages for a company in St. Paul in 1874. He worked hard and used the math skills he learned at school on the job. He soon became an **accountant**. Accountants keep track of money for businesses. John worked at the same company for 51 years. His son John, Jr., was an early African American lawyer in Minnesota.

When William Grey and John Hickman arrived in Minnesota, fewer than 300 African Americans lived here. By the time they were teenagers, more than 1,500 African Americans made Minnesota their home. Although they took different journeys and came for different reasons, the Greys and the Hickmans helped build the African American community and their state. William and his family worked in the abolition movement in Minneapolis. John and his family helped build a strong church community in St. Paul. They also helped black men get the right to vote in their state. Minnesota might be very different if the Grey and Hickman families hadn't moved here 150 years ago.

JOHN H. HICKMAN, SR.

AUDITOR IS GIVEN PENSION AFTER 51 YEARS' SERVICE

John Hickman retired from the firm of Finch, Van Slycke, and McConville in 1924, after 51 years of service as an accountant and auditor.

Meet Mattie McIntosh

When Mattie McIntosh was growing up, girls wore dresses with long skirts, high necks, and lots of buttons.

Mattie McIntosh was born in 1887 and grew up in Minneapolis, but she would probably not recognize the city today with its shiny skyscrapers and busy freeways. But Mattie could tell you about the river that runs through the city, the Mississippi. Many things have changed since Mattie was a girl, but the strong Mississippi River still flows through our state's biggest city.

Mattie's family lived in northeast Minneapolis, about six blocks from the river. They could get almost everything they needed right in their **neighborhood**. Mattie could walk to school, to the grocery store, to the park, and to church. Her father could even walk to work. Mattie could also walk to the river and listen to the sounds of people working along the Mississippi.

Mattie McIntosh grew up near the Mississippi River in Northeast Minneapolis. This map shows the boundaries of St. Paul and Minneapolis today.

Mattie's Work at Home

Mattie had 10 brothers and sisters. The McIntosh house was probably a two-story wooden house like many older homes you can still find in Minnesota.

Keeping up a house took a lot of work when Mattie was a girl. Most homes in Minnesota didn't have elec-

Most houses in the late 1800s used wood stoves like the one below for cooking and heating.

tricity then. Instead, families used lamps lit by **kerosene**, a special oil that burns. Most houses didn't have gas or electric stoves. Instead, families burned wood in their stoves for both cooking and heating. Many homes didn't have an indoor toilet. Instead, they had to use one outside called an outhouse. At night, people used chamber pots hidden under their beds if they didn't want to walk to the outhouse.

Keeping up a house in the late 1800s included cleaning the glass on kerosene lamps, squeezing rinse water out of clothes with a hand wringer, and emptying the chamber pot.

Mattie McIntosh probably went to Everett School in Minneapolis, shown here in the late 1880s.

Kids like Mattie had many chores to do around the house. Some had to clean the kerosene lamps and empty ashes out of the wood-burning stoves. Others had to cut, stack, and carry wood. Someone also had to empty and wash the chamber pots every morning.

Mattie's Work at School

In Minneapolis 100 years ago schools were open to all students, both black and white. The school nearest Mattie's house was Everett School, so it's likely Mattie went there.

In the 1890s, just as today, students in Minneapolis went to school from September until June. Grade school started at 9:00 a.m. At noon, schools closed so students could go home to eat lunch. Sometimes kids stopped at nearby stores to buy treats, such as lime hard candies, rubber chewing gum, and pickles. Students returned to school at 1:30 p.m. and stayed until 3:30 p.m.

Black and white children attended school together more than 100 years ago.

When Mattie was in fourth grade, Minneapolis students studied numbers, reading, spelling, sewing, plants and animals, geography, mapping, writing, drawing, music, and physical exercises.

Mattie at Play

When Mattie wasn't doing chores at home or going to school, she and her brothers and sisters probably played just like kids today. Kids growing up in Minneapolis in the 1890s enjoyed many games. Boys often played marbles and went fishing. Girls often played with dolls and jacks. Many kids also admired a new **invention**—the bicycle!

Families in Minnesota enjoyed picnicking by the Mississippi 100 years ago. Kids took off their shoes and long stockings to wade in the cool water. Mattie's daughter remembered going to picnics at Minnehaha Falls in Minneapolis. The McIntoshes may have gone there for picnics when Mattie was a girl, too.

School rules were very strict back then. If you were late two times in one month, the school suspended you! If you were absent for three days in a row, you needed special permission from the principal to get back into school. At the end of every year, students in Mattie's class took a test. If they passed the test, they could move up to the next grade. If they didn't, they had to stay in the same grade.

Mattie may have played with a doll like this Cuban doll from the 1880s.

Mattie's Father's Work at the Sawmill

The Mississippi River wasn't just a place for neighborhood families. It was also a place to work. Many **mills** lined the river in downtown Minneapolis. The flour mills turned wheat into flour. The sawmills turned logs into **lumber**. When Mattie was a girl, the mills were very busy and very noisy.

Lumbermen sent logs down the Mississippi River to St. Anthony to be turned into lumber at the sawmills.

Mattie's father and other African Americans worked in the lumber **industry**. Mr. McIntosh had a job at the W. C. Stetson sawmill in Minneapolis. This mill was on the Mississippi River, only six blocks away from Mattie's house.

Lumberjacks in northern Minnesota cut down trees and floated the logs down the Mississippi River to Minneapolis. Workers caught the logs in the river with long poles and brought them to the mills. In the mills, machines turned the logs into lumber. Finally, builders used the lumber to make buildings and houses all over the country.

Mr. McIntosh held many different jobs at the sawmill. One of his jobs there was as a teamster. He had to hook up a team of horses to a wagon and carry logs and lumber.

Mattie's Mother's Work at Fort Snelling

Mattie's mother also worked on the Mississippi River but not at the mills. She worked at Fort Snelling. The fort sits on a hill overlooking the spot where the Minnesota and Mississippi rivers join.

When Mattie's grandparents moved to Minnesota in the 1860s, they lived on the Minnesota River near Fort Snelling. Her daughter grew up hearing stories about Mattie's grandparents canoeing across the river to trade at the fort. Mattie also told her daughter a story about the time her grandparents traded for oranges at Fort Snelling. Mattie's family believes these oranges were poisoned, and that her grandparents died from eating them.

When Mattie was a girl, her mother cooked and cleaned at Fort Snelling. To get to work from Northeast Minneapolis, Mrs. McIntosh probably took a trolley driven by horses. Her trolley crossed a bridge over the Mississippi River into downtown Minneapolis and continued by land all the way to the fort.

Minnesota African Americans in Mattie's Day

Mattie's family was just one of many African American families living in Minnesota. The number of blacks in Minnesota grew quickly when Mattie was a girl. In 1880 about 1,500 blacks lived in Minnesota. Twenty years later, when Mattie was 13, almost 5,000 blacks lived here. This was because African Americans in Minnesota

Mr. McIntosh worked at a sawmill like this one, near downtown Minneapolis.

John Q. Adams moved to Minnesota to run The Appeal *newspaper. He lived in this house in St. Paul.*

invited blacks from other parts of the country to move here.

One of these newcomers was a writer named John Quincy Adams. He moved to St. Paul, where he ran an African American newspaper called *The Appeal*. It reported on events in the African American community. It even included a kids' corner where stories and letters written by children were printed. *The Appeal* also wrote about African Americans struggling for equality. By the time Mattie was in fourth grade, African Americans all around the country read *The Appeal*.

Struggling for Equality

When Mattie was nine, the U.S. Supreme Court made a decision that would make life harder for African Americans for many years. The Supreme Court makes decisions about laws for everyone in the country. In 1896 the court listened to a case involving Homer Plessy and John Howard Ferguson.

Mr. Plessy was an African American man who refused to leave a whites-only train car in Louisiana. He wanted the court to decide that blacks have the right to sit anywhere on trains. Mr. Ferguson was a judge in the state of Louisiana. He wanted the court to decide that Louisiana could separate blacks and whites on trains. The Supreme Court agreed it was legal to separate, or **segregate**, whites and blacks in public places such as trains, schools, and restrooms.

In Minnesota, African Americans worked together to help blacks in states that segregated people. They wrote newspaper articles asking for equality, and they spoke to people in the government. Once they raised money to send a black man from Minnesota to protest by riding on a whites-only train in Tennessee.

John Cheatham was the first African American fire-fighter in Minneapolis. Mr. Cheatham was Mattie's uncle. He later became a fire captain.

Segregation was illegal in Minnesota when Mattie was growing up, but it was not always easy for African Americans here, either. Some local restaurants and hotels refused to serve them. For

Amanda Lyles was an African American businesswoman. She also was active in the struggle for civil rights.

example, one restaurant in St. Paul wouldn't serve an African American artist named William Hazel. But Mr. Hazel didn't take "no" for an answer.

Through the courts in Minnesota, he fought the restaurant for the right to eat there. Not only did he win, but the court also said the restaurant had to pay

MEMBERS OF THE AFRO-AMERICAN COUNCIL, IN SESSION AT ST. PAUL.

Rt. Rev. Alexander Walters, of New Jersey, is in the Center of the Front Row, and Booker T. Washington Stands at His Right. Mrs. Ida Wells Barnett Stands at President Walter's Left.

The National Afro-American Council was started with the help of African Americans in Minnesota. They worked to gain civil rights for African Americans around the country. In 1902 the council held a national conference in St. Paul.

him $24 because it had been unfair— a large sum at the time.

Women in Minnesota also helped fight for equality. One was Amanda Lyles, an African American who owned a beauty shop and funeral parlor in St. Paul. In 1897 Mrs. Lyles went to the first national African American women's **conference** in Tennessee and gave a speech there.

In 1902, when Mattie was 15, the National Afro-American Council held a meeting in St. Paul. Hundreds of people from around the country came, including famous African American leaders such as Booker T. Washington and Ida B. Wells-Barnett. We don't know for sure if Mattie or her parents attended the conference, but we can be sure many Minnesotans were proud that this important meeting was held in their state.

Mattie Grows Up

When Mattie grew up, she got married, had three children, and worked at Fort Snelling like her mother. Can you imagine the changes Mattie saw in her lifetime? She saw plumbing and electricity come into people's homes. She saw changes in people's jobs, too. By the time she was an older woman, many of the busy mills on the river had closed. Mattie also saw the end of the laws that segregated blacks and whites. Now all Americans can ride trains and go to school together.

Some people who attended the 1902 Afro-American Council conference in St. Paul received this badge.

Meet Nellie Stone Johnson

Nellie Stone Johnson, upper right, was the oldest child in her family. She was about 10 years old when this photograph was taken.

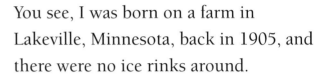

Ice-skating was one of my favorite things to do when I was growing up. But I could not walk to the nearest **ice rink**, put on my skates, and glide across the rink like kids do today. First, I had to make my own ice rink.

You see, I was born on a farm in Lakeville, Minnesota, back in 1905, and there were no ice rinks around.

On snowy days, I used to go out to the barn and get my horse. Then I attached a **road slip**—a square metal tool—to the horse. Next my horse and I rode off to the pond near our farmhouse. We would ride up and down the pond, dragging the road slip and pulling the snow off the pond. When the ice peeked out from beneath the snow, it was finally time to skate.

My name is Nellie Stone Johnson, and I'm

Nellie rode her horse for fun and for farm chores.

telling you my own story. Now I'm 92 years old. Clearing the snow off the pond wasn't the only thing my horse and I did when I was growing up on the farm. We kept busy all year round. In the summers, my horse and I delivered a newspaper called the *Nonpartisan Leader* to farmers in our area. The *Leader* **encouraged** farmers to work together to get good prices for their crops. In the fall, we carried corn from the fields to feed the cows.

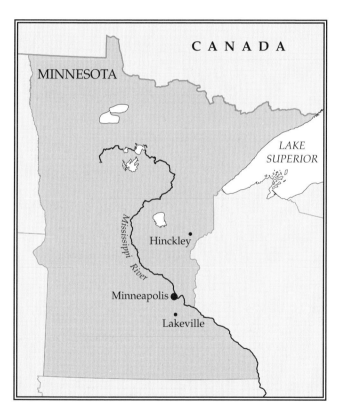

Nellie Stone Johnson was born on a farm near Lakeville, Minnesota. Later, her family moved to a larger farm near Hinckley. When Nellie was a teenager, she moved to Minneapolis to continue her education.

Nellie's Family Starts a Farm

Before I was born, my parents moved north to Minnesota to find new jobs. My mother was a schoolteacher who came to Minnesota from Kentucky and Chicago. My father was a farmer from Missouri. They met at church in Minneapolis. After they got married, my parents decided to start a farm.

Our family raised **dairy** cows. We made our living selling the milk to a company in Minneapolis. First we poured the milk into big cans. Then we sent the milk cans to Minneapolis. Sometimes the dairy company in Minneapolis cheated farmers by not paying for all the milk. My family helped start a new dairy company that paid dairy farmers fairly. Later this small company grew into Land O'Lakes. You might have heard of it.

We had many animals on our farm. We owned cows, horses, pigs, and chickens. We raised many crops, such as oats, corn, wheat, and potatoes. My family also had huge vegetable gardens. Our gardens were so big that my mother cooked and canned hundreds of jars of vegetables every fall. We ate the canned vegetables all through the long winter months. I believe I have lived so long and am so healthy because of the fresh food we ate on the farm and because I always drank milk.

Nellie Does Her Chores

Working on the farm with my horse wasn't the only chore I had growing up. Neither my father nor my mother believed that boys' work should be different from girls' work. I did chores both inside and outside. In the house, I helped my mother with cooking, cleaning, washing, and ironing. It wasn't easy! In those days we did not have modern washing machines. We didn't even have electricity!

Outside, I helped my father in the barn with the cows. Every morning, all year long, my father started his day at 5:00 a.m. I got out of bed around 6:00 a.m., put on my heavy overalls and shirt, and went out to the barn to milk the cows. When I was only six, I learned how to milk a cow by practicing on a very gentle one named Spot. The better I got, the more cows I milked. By the time I was in high school, I milked 30 cows every day, including Sundays.

After chores, I'd go back inside the house to change into my school clothes and eat breakfast. On warm days, I wore a cotton dress with a **pinafore**—an apron that helps keep your dress clean.

Families saved fruits and vegetables from their garden in jars like this one. They ate canned goods during the long winter months when fresh food was scarce.

Nellie's family owned one of the earliest cars, a Model T Ford.

In the winter, I wore my pinafore with a wool dress to stay warm. I liked the big pockets in my pinafore. I usually carried a pocketknife in case I needed to fix something. After breakfast on Sundays we would drive our Model T Ford to church.

On school days, I walked two miles to a one-room schoolhouse. Just one teacher taught all the children from kindergarten all the way to eighth grade. I liked our one-room schoolhouse because I could learn more. You see,

Nellie wore overalls to milk cows. Then she changed into a dress and a pinafore for school.

I used to listen to my own lessons *and* the lessons the older kids were studying. By the time I was in seventh grade, I was teaching math at school.

This photo was taken around 1910. Nellie went to a one-room schoolhouse like this one, which was near Fergus Falls, Minnesota.

Nellie Learns about Politics

When I was young, I really enjoyed school, and I loved reading. My favorite present at Christmas was a new book. At school, I started a student group to help our farm families. It was called the Little Citizen's League. I was the president. We did things like deliver a newspaper to farmers in our area. When I was in eighth grade, I even taught my school a lesson on our government's **politics**. Politics is the way people work together to run the government. Everyone can be a part of it. Delivering those newspapers was one way I was a part of it—even as a young person.

I learned a lot about politics from my family. After long days of work and school and play, my family gathered to eat dinner together. We always talked about politics at dinner. We talked about things like how the government treated farmers and African Americans.

I also watched my father. He was an important role model for me. For example, he wanted to help improve schools in our area. So he decided to run for a seat on the school board in Dakota County. School boards make important decisions about how schools are run. My father was the first African American to be elected to a school board in Minnesota.

Reading the newspaper was another way I learned about politics. I read it every day. In fact, I read two newspapers each day. My family took the *Minneapolis Morning Tribune* and the *Chicago Defender*. They were both important

papers, but the *Defender* wrote about Africans and African Americans all over the world. The *Tribune* didn't write about African Americans very often, but it did let us know what was happening in Minnesota.

One of the stories I read in the Minneapolis newspaper was about a Minnesota **lynching**—the murder of a person by a large group. In 1920 a large group of white men lynched three African Americans in Duluth. These young men had been falsely accused of harming a white woman. Before the trial, the white men dragged the three black men from their jail cells. Then

Three African Americans were lynched in Duluth in 1920, when Nellie was 15. As an adult, Nellie worked hard to pass laws to protect African Americans.

The Minneapolis Morning Tribune

Fifty-fourth Year. No. 23.   Associated Press   MINNEAPOLIS, MINN., WEDNESDAY, JUNE 16, 1920   United Press   Price Two Cents in Minneapolis

Duluth Mob Hangs 3 Negroes to Avenge Young Girl; 3 Freed By Lynch Law Court Held in Battered Jail

Nellie moved to Minneapolis to finish high school and attend the University of Minnesota, pictured here in 1905.

they hanged the men from a light pole on the streets of Duluth. I had read about lynchings of African Americans in other parts of the country before, but this was the first time it happened in Minnesota.

Nellie Moves to Minneapolis

About the same time as the Duluth lynchings, I had to make a hard choice. I wanted to finish high school, but the one closest to our farm was 14 miles away, in Hinckley. That made for a long horseback ride every morning and every afternoon! My aunt and uncle in Minneapolis said I could move in with them and go to a high school near their home. I decided to move to Minneapolis. I finished high school there and started college at the University of Minnesota.

As a young adult, I kept on studying hard and working in politics. When I was in college, I worked at the Minneapolis Athletic Club. I helped form a group for the African American workers there. Our new group worked hard to help us get pay raises, vacation time, and better jobs. That was my first of many **victories** in politics.

Later, I helped women make the same amount of money as the men at work. I also joined a political group called the Farmer-Labor Party. Some of

Nellie Stone Johnson ran her own sewing business for many years in downtown Minneapolis.

Nellie Helps Make a Better World

As I look back on my life, I can see that my education and my experiences gave me many skills to help make life better in Minnesota for farmers, women, and African Americans.

There are many ways to get an education. Mine started at home. My parents taught me to work hard on the farm and for our community of farmers. I learned how to read, write, and do math at the schools I attended. In politics, I learned how to improve jobs and make better laws for people in our state.

I think the best education is a combination of what you learn in the classroom and what you learn from doing things yourself. You need to test what you learn at school in the real world. And the world isn't

Nellie Stone Johnson, far right, was a member of the National Association for the Advancement of Colored People (NAACP). The NAACP has fought for equal rights since the early 1900s.

us worked with the Democratic Party to form the Democratic-Farmer-Labor (DFL) Party. A national anti-lynching law was one goal of the new DFL party. I worked with Minnesota DFL Senator Hubert H. Humphrey to pass new laws to protect African Americans.

going to be a better place if you just sit around and talk. You've got to get out there and work! Here's how I like to put it:

If you've got to plow a field, get out there and plow that field, and do it in the way it's supposed to be done. No amount of words are going to make the plow go down into the earth.

When Nellie was young, farmers still used plows pulled by horses. The plows turned up the dirt for planting.

Meet James Griffin

You might say my life changed for good in 1929, the year I turned 12 years old. That was the year the Hallie Q. Brown Community House opened up in my neighborhood in St. Paul. Hallie Q. was a place where African Americans got together

HALLIE Q. BROWN COMMUNITY HOUSE

Volunteer **AWARD** Leadership

PRESENTED TO

James Griffin
May 3, 1956

in recognition and appreciation of volunteer service in assisting with special events during the year. The value of the services given are without measure to the participants and to the community.

John M. Patton
The Board of Directors of
Hallie Q. Brown House

James Griffin played football and basketball at the Hallie Q. Brown House in St. Paul. Many years later, he received an award for his work as an adult volunteer there.

to have fun and learn new things. It was one of the first centers for blacks in Minnesota. If you were a grown-up, you could go to Hallie Q. for dances and parties. And if you were 12 years old, you could join a real sports team there.

I got a lot of exercise as a kid. I walked two miles to school and two miles home again every day. I played with the Irish and German kids who lived on my block. In the winters, we'd skate at the ice rink nearby, too. But I had never joined a real team before I was 12. When Hallie Q. opened, I joined the new football and basketball teams. Sports changed my life.

I loved playing, so I worked hard. Soon I was good enough to play for a citywide basketball team. After high school, I won a sports **scholarship** to a college in West Virginia. When I returned to Minnesota, I played for a semipro basketball team that traveled all over the Midwest. Later I wrote about

Teenagers in St. Paul's Summit-University neighborhood enjoyed skating on nearby rinks.

sports for a newspaper called the *St. Paul Recorder.*

Now that I'm older, I don't play sports very often. But I still encourage young people to play sports. Kids must

James Griffin started his police career as a patrol officer in 1941 and retired as deputy chief in 1983.

learn how to work together. When you work together, you can **accomplish** a lot—for yourself and for your team.

James Griffin Becomes a Police Officer

Traveling as a basketball player didn't pay much, so I tried to find a job. I decided to take the tests to be a police officer. It wasn't easy to get the job back then. First of all, I was African American, and the city didn't hire many blacks. Second, it was in the 1930s during the Great Depression, and many people were out of work. At one point, even the city of St. Paul couldn't afford to hire new police officers for two years.

To become a police officer, I had to take three tests: a written test, a physical test, and a medical test. I passed the written and the physical tests right away. Passing the medical test was more

difficult. I took it three times, because the doctors kept failing me. Once I failed because one of my toes overlaps another toe! When I checked it out with my own doctor, he said I was fine. I knew then that I had been **discriminated** against.

I didn't pass the medical test until I visited the father of a friend of mine, Mr. Axel Peterson. He was on the St. Paul city council. After he listened to my story, Mr. Peterson said he'd see what he could do. About a week later, I went back to take that medical test again. All of a sudden, I passed with flying colors and was finally hired as a police officer in 1941.

My first job on the force was as a patrolman. I walked around low-income neighborhoods near downtown St. Paul to make sure everything was safe on my **beat**. Over the years, I worked all over the city. Back then, you worked for seven days in a row and had the eighth day off. You also had to buy your own uniform.

In the St. Paul police department, there weren't many opportunities for black officers to receive promotions. But we knew that **veterans**—people who served in the armed forces—had a good chance at getting promoted.

James Griffin Joins the U.S. Navy

When I joined the St. Paul police department, many countries around the world were fighting in World War II. After a friend talked to me, I enlisted in the U.S. Navy. I was a dry-land sailor. That means I never shipped out to sea, because the war was winding down. But I was in the navy for over a year.

Now, in my day, the navy and the army were segregated, or separated by race. That means they had white camps and black camps. Most of the African

American recruits knew that, but some of the white Americans didn't.

Before leaving Minnesota, all the new sailors were out at Fort Snelling for about 10 days. I got to be friends with an Irish guy named Jim Cunningham. He was from up on the Iron Range. We kind of hit it off, and do you know what he said to me? He said, "Jim, we'll stay

James Griffin served in the United States Navy at the end of World War II.

together until this thing is over and we'll come back home."

I laughed and said, "You don't understand."

"What do you mean?" he asked.

"When we leave Fort Snelling," I answered, "I'll never see you again until this war is over."

"Why not?"

"We'll be segregated, because you're white and I'm black."

Cunningham didn't believe me, but I was right. After we left Minnesota, I didn't see him again until after the war.

James Griffin Sees a Noose

The United States ended segregation in the navy at the end of World War II. I know because I was there. My company was in training in Illinois at an all-black camp called Camp Smalls. I'll never forget the day we were marching up and down in the hot sun. A young man came over and told us we needed to stop marching and report to the **barracks**, or basic housing for the military.

When we got to the barracks, one of the officers came down to read a statement from the head of the U.S. Navy. It went something like this: "As of this day, segregation in the United States Navy training will end. Your company will stay intact. But you'll be shipped out of Camp Smalls to Camp Downs to finish your training there. The new group that is being formed here today will be the last all-black company formed in the United States Navy."

Well, Camp Downs had been an all-white camp very near Camp Smalls. We were the first black company to arrive there. When we got to Camp Downs, it was time to eat. Our company walked to the chow hall, or cafeteria. When we were all sitting down with our food, one of our men asked, "Did you see that up there?"

We all looked up and saw a **noose**—a long rope with a round loop at one end—hanging from the ceiling. Our leader snatched a couple of big guys and said, "Cut that thing down." So they did. Then he said, "You guys just go on eating. I'll be back."

Then our leader left to talk to the officer of the day. Our leader said, "We came here peaceably. They've got a noose hanging up in the chow hall. I controlled it today, but if this continues, I don't know if I can. If you don't do something about that, we might have a riot here."

The officer put an end to the problem, and we never had any more trouble at Camp Downs.

James Griffin Wins at Home

When I returned home to Minnesota after the war, I continued working for the St. Paul police department. Being a veteran helped me move up and get promotions. But I still had challenges. One of the biggest challenges I ever had was becoming deputy chief.

The head of the police department is the chief of police. St. Paul has several deputy chiefs who work for the chief.

CIVIL SERVICE BUREAU
CITY OF ST. PAUL

NOTICE OF EXAMINATION RATING

This is to notify you that you attained a passing mark in the examination for
Deputy Chief of Police

held __July 12, 1972__ . Your name is No. ___1___ on the original entrance list.

CIVIL SERVICE BUREAU

Mr. James S. Griffin

Report of your ratings

Subject		Wt.	Product
DIRECT EXAM.	91.40	60	5484.00
Service Rating	84.00	30	2520.00
Seniority	100.00	10	1000.00
		100)	9004.00
		FINAL AVERAGE:	90.04

SUNSET FINAL

St. Paul Dispatch

Today's Closing N.Y. Stock Quotes

3 p.m. temperature 94   56 PAGES   ST. PAUL, MINN., THURSDAY, AUGUST 17, 1972   PRICE 10 CENTS

GRIFFIN ELEVATED TO DEPUTY CHIEF

James Griffin scored the highest on the deputy chief's examination (top), but he didn't get the job. He challenged the decision and was promoted to deputy chief in 1972 (bottom).

Now, the first black police officer joined the St. Paul police department in 1881, but St. Paul had never hired an African American supervisor before I came on board. I was the first sergeant and the first captain in St. Paul. When one of the deputy chief jobs opened up, I decided to apply for it, too. I had to take another test. I don't mind telling you that I had the highest score. But I was black. They gave the job to the man with the second-highest score. He was white.

Now I knew this wasn't right. So I called up a lawyer named Doug Thomson to challenge the appointment. Guess what? I got that job after all. I was the first African American deputy chief in St. Paul.

James Griffin Helps Build a Strong Community

I don't want to give you the idea that my life has been nothing but struggles. I

James Griffin retired from the police force in 1983 after 42 years of service.

was born and raised right here in Minnesota. I'm proud I raised my children here, too. Part of what has made Minnesota a good home is that we have a strong community. To make a strong community, you've got to participate in it. You've got to be part of the team.

My parents showed me how to be involved in the community. They talked about the community and Minnesota at

Griffin's mother worked on election days. She counted ballots collected in a voting box like the one above.

Griffin's father worked as a dining car waiter for the railroad. He may have worn a uniform like the ones these Northern Pacific Railway waiters were wearing in the early 1940s.

The stadium at Central High School in St. Paul was renamed for James Griffin in 1988. This is a headline from the St. Paul Public School Staff Reporter.

the dinner table. My mother worked at the voting booths on election day. When my father was away working on the railroad, he always mailed in his election ballot.

When I grew up, I wanted to participate in the community, too. I've never missed but four or five elections since I was old enough to vote, and I'm not a young man. I was elected to and served on the St. Paul school board for 17 years. I also **refereed** games in more than 30 high schools and colleges all over this state.

All my sports, police work, and community work paid off. A few years ago the football field at my old high school was named after me—the James S. Griffin Stadium at Central High School in St. Paul.

If you want to succeed, you've got to work hard. You've got to stay in school, you've got to make friendships and work together with people, and you've got to give back a little of what you were given. You can say James Griffin told you so!

James Griffin relaxes at home with his family in the 1950s. Pictured from left to right are: Vianne, Edna, James, Helen, and Linda Griffin.

Meet David Taylor

"Fire!" screamed David Taylor's parents. They were watching in shock as their nine-year-old son raced down the hill in a **pushcart** with flames shooting out from underneath.

That blazing pushcart was just one of many projects designed by David and his creative friends. They made the cart from an old wooden radio cabinet and from the wheels on some metal roller skates. David and his friend pulled the pushcart to the top of a hill and the two of them climbed in. Then they started down the hill.

As the cart picked up speed, the metal wheels rubbed against the wood, causing sparks that turned to flames. David's parents watched in horror as the pushcart sped down the hill with the flames growing larger. As the boys reached the bottom of the hill and the wheels slowed, the flames died down. When the cart slowed down, David and his friend jumped out to safety.

Growing up in Summit-University

David grew up in a neighborhood called Summit-University in the 1950s. He lived with his mother, his stepfather, and his two brothers. Many of the families living in Summit-University were African American. Most of them also shared similar values and beliefs. The neighborhood was like one large **extended** family.

Summit-University also had almost everything that people in the community needed. There were shops, stores, churches, a community center, friends, and relatives right near David's house. He could walk wherever he needed to go. Everyone knew David's grandfather because he walked around the neighborhood so much. His nickname was "Walking Joe Vassar."

David had to follow many rules growing up in his neighborhood. There

The Summit-University neighborhood is in central St. Paul.

David Taylor (bottom) as a boy with his mother and his two brothers.

The Summit-University neighborhood had many shops, like this small grocery store.

neighborhood watched out for the children. The adults protected the children, and told parents if they saw children break any rules. Many of these watchful neighbors were called "Aunt" and "Uncle," even though they were not related by blood.

David and his friends had to follow a city rule every night, too. They had to be home by 8:00 p.m., even on weekends.

When the Interstate 94 freeway was built, it went right through Summit-University. The neighborhood changed. Houses, stores, and even playgrounds were torn down to make way for the new freeway. Many families felt the loss of their strong community.

were family rules, community rules, and city rules. At home, David was expected to stay neat and clean all day. He had to behave properly and speak correct English all the time. "Behaving properly" meant speaking with respect to every adult, attending church every Sunday, completing his daily chores at home, and getting good grades in school.

David also had to follow community rules. Most of the adults in David's

David at Maxfield Elementary School

One of the buildings that had to be torn down for the new freeway was David's school. He went to the old Maxfield Elementary School until fourth grade. It was made of dark red brick and was two stories tall. But the school was very old and in poor shape. David said it could have gone up in flames like his pushcart.

One day when David was in the third grade, a storm came up while he sat in class. He and some of his classmates saw the window and frame being pushed in by strong winds. They yelled, and everyone ran to the other side of

Students participate in a music lesson at the old Maxfield Elementary School.

Many people's homes and businesses were torn down when the I-94 freeway construction started in the 1950s.

David attended fifth and sixth grade in the new Maxfield Elementary School, pictured above.

Another Struggle over Schools

Around the same time, two parents in another African American community wanted their child to attend school in their own neighborhood, too. In Topeka, Kansas, a third-grade African American girl named Linda Brown had to walk one mile and cross a dangerous railroad yard to reach her all-black school. Her parents wanted Linda to go to a school only seven blocks away from home. This school was all white. Linda's father asked the Topeka school board if his daughter could attend the nearby school for whites. They said she couldn't because she was black.

Mr. Brown would not take "no" for an answer. He found help at the National Association for the Advancement of Colored People (NAACP). This group works to improve the lives of African Americans and other people of color.

the room. As they ran, the window, frame and all, crashed down onto their seats.

Soon after the storm, St. Paul decided to build a new Maxfield Elementary School. But where? Everyone agreed that it had to be away from the path of the new freeway. Many parents in the African American community wanted the new Maxfield School to stay in the Summit-University neighborhood.

The Browns and the NAACP worked for Linda's right to go to the all-white school near her house. They took the case all the way to the U.S. Supreme Court.

The Supreme Court makes decisions about laws for everyone in the country. In 1896 the court decided it was legal to have separate schools for blacks and whites. This was still the law when the Browns were trying to get permission to send Linda to the all-white school.

After listening to the Browns' story, the Supreme Court decided the 1896 law had been wrong. In a 1954 decision called *Brown versus Board of Education of Topeka*, *Kansas* the Supreme Court decided school segregation was illegal. Linda Brown could finally go to the school near her house.

In St. Paul, one year after that decision, the new Maxfield School opened right in David's neighborhood, next to the new freeway. Thanks to the **efforts** of the parents in his neighborhood, David Taylor attended fifth and sixth grades at the new Maxfield School.

Rosa Parks and Dr. Martin Luther King, Jr.

Getting a new, safer school built in David's neighborhood was not the only thing that happened after *Brown versus Board of Education*. The courage of Linda Brown and her family **inspired** many people all over the country. For example, in those days blacks in the South were supposed to sit in the back of the bus and give up their seats to white people if the bus got full. One day, a young woman named Rosa Parks refused to give up her seat to a white man in Montgomery, Alabama. She was arrested and put in jail. After that, many people in Montgomery refused to ride buses. Instead, they walked

Roy Wilkins was national head of the National Association for the Advancement of Colored People (NAACP) for 22 years. He helped pass many civil rights acts in the 1950s and 1960s. Wilkins grew up in St. Paul and graduated from the University of Minnesota.

Martin Luther King, Jr. and Rosa Parks

Dr. King inspired many people to join in the struggle. One of those he inspired was David Taylor. In 1962 Dr. King came to Minnesota to give a speech. After the speech, David went backstage to meet him. By his example, Dr. King showed David that every person could help make the world a better place.

Making a Difference with a Newspaper

When David Taylor was growing up, he didn't watch much TV. He liked school, he liked sports, and he liked reading. David often read as many as 10 books in two weeks!

He also liked playing with his friends. David and his friends formed a club. They built many clubhouses. Some of these were underground. Some were made from old chicken houses. They also built pushcarts like the one that went up in flames.

to work, and the bus company lost money.

Dr. Martin Luther King, Jr., helped organize this battle against the city bus company in Montgomery. It was the first of many times he led thousands of people in peaceful **demonstrations**. He wanted to improve the lives of African Americans and change unfair laws in the United States.

When David was 10, his club wanted to make some money. They decided to start their own newspaper. The boys got an old **typewriter**, and they made an office in the attic of one club member's house. The boys **interviewed** people in the community and wrote stories about them. They sold ads to local businesses. David drew cartoons for the newspaper.

The boys also printed jokes in their newspaper, like this one: A girl asks a boy how he likes school. The boy answers, "Closed!" Or this one: A waiter asks a customer why he's not eating his fish dinner. The man answers, "Long time, no sea!"

David and his friends published their newspaper once a week for two years. They sold it all around the neighborhood. Sometimes, they sold 75 copies in a week. Their paper cost three cents a copy. So the boys made up to $2.25 a week. Both kids and grown-ups enjoyed the paper. David and his friends made a

In the 1960s, African Americans still could not eat in many restaurants in some parts of the United States. In Minnesota, people demonstrated peacefully to show their support for blacks in other parts of the country.

contribution to their community through their newspaper.

Becoming a Historian

Making a newspaper and reading lots of books are just two examples of David's curious mind. He was also a very good student. But school and the community were not the only places David used his mind. He also studied at home. He asked his relatives many questions about their family history. He learned that there were some very important people among his ancestors, or relatives from a long time ago. One of them was former U.S. President Benjamin Harrison!

David Taylor and his friends wrote and published the Weekly Trumpet, *a neighborhood newspaper, for two years.*

Eula Vassar Taylor Murphy, David Taylor's mother, is pictured above.

David's curiosity about his family started his love of history. He decided to study history in college. He wrote a book on his family history and many articles about African Americans in Minnesota. Now David works where he can share his love of history. He became a history professor and an administrator at the University of Minnesota.

Like the historians in Africa—the **griots** (*GREE-ohs*)—David knows the importance of remembering the past. Stories about people in our past can inspire and encourage us today. They also help us remember the past correctly. Starting with his newspaper at age 10, David Taylor made sure that people would know the facts about his community. Now he is a modern-day griot.

A West African griot instructs his students.

Meet Eric Mosley and Mahamoud Aden Amin

"Sweet potato pie? Why should *I* make **sweet potato** pie?" asks 10-year-old Eric Mosley, shaking his head. "That's the only kind of pie my grandmother makes!"

Eric is walking down a long, sunny hall at the Minnesota History Center in St. Paul. It is a Sunday afternoon in January 1999. Eric is here to celebrate the birthday of Martin Luther King, Jr. To be honest, Eric would rather be at home watching the Vikings play football on TV. But he is here to watch a play about Dr. King. The play doesn't start for 30 minutes. Since he must wait, Eric agrees to make a **traditional** African American dessert, sweet potato pie, in the crafts room.

As Eric turns into the yellow crafts room, he sees he's not the only guy missing the Vikings. He spies three boys sitting at a table. They are putting **piecrust** into small tin cups.

A woman from the History Center gives Eric a cup and the food he needs to make his pie. Then Eric turns around to look for a place to sit.

Eric Mosley enjoys a snowy afternoon in Minnesota.

Mahamoud Aden Amin (middle) laughs with his older brothers Mohamed (left) and Ahmed (right).

Eric Makes a New Friend

"Mind if I join you?" Eric asks the three boys.

"No problem," answers the youngest boy. "What's your name?"

"I'm Eric. Eric Mosley."

"Hi! My name is Mahamoud Aden Amin (*Mah-HA-mood AH-deen AH-meen*). These two guys are my big brothers."

"Hi there! Do you like sweet potato pie?" asks Eric.

"I don't know. I've never had sweet potato pie before," says Mahamoud.

"What? You've never eaten sweet potato pie? I've eaten it a hundred times. Where have you been?"

"We're from Somalia (*So-MAH-lee-ya*)," answers Mahamoud as he mixes some butter into a bowl of cooked sweet potatoes. "We don't eat sweet potato pie in Somalia."

"Really? What do you eat there?"

Eric and Mahamoud make sweet potato pie.

"Lots of stuff. Especially lots of fresh meats, fruits, and vegetables the farmers sell in the market."

"Cool. So, how old are you, Mahamoud?"

"I'm 10, and I'm in fourth grade."

"Really?" answers Eric, "Me, too!"

Eric and Mahamoud continue talking as they work on the sweet potato pies.

Mahamoud Escapes from Somalia

"So why did your family leave Somalia?"

"There was a war in Somalia. It was dangerous. My father didn't think it was safe for us anymore."

"A war? Did you ever see any guns or anything?" asks Eric as he stirs an egg into the sweet potatoes.

"I've seen guns. I remember seeing a lot of guns when we escaped from our home in Mogadishu (*Mo-ga-DEE-shoo*). Many Somalis left the country and went to **refugee** camps in the south. But my father took us to his family home in northern Somalia. We had to take a bus through the country of Ethiopia (*EE-thee-OH-pee-a*) to get to northern Somalia. An army general and his soldiers **guarded** our bus. All those guys had guns."

"That's serious. But how come you're here now? Wasn't it safe in northern Somalia either?"

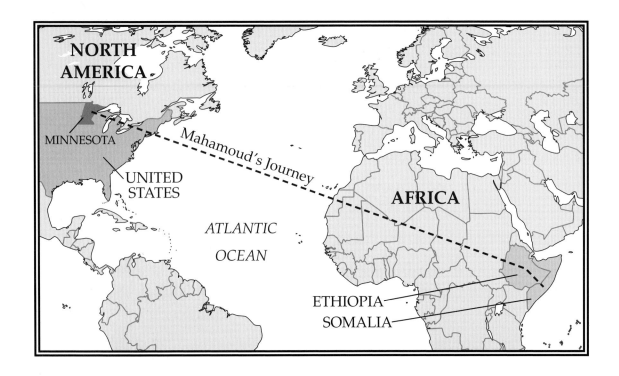

Mahamoud was born in Somalia in East Africa. His family escaped from Somalia to come to the United States in 1996.

Eric's ancestors, or family from a long time ago, also came from Africa. They were taken from their homes in West Africa and brought to the United States, probably to work as slaves, about 200 years ago. Mahamoud explains that his family left Africa only a few years ago.

"Well, it was safer, but there were still problems. It was hard to find food and water. There were no schools. My father wanted us to go to school."

"So what did you do?" asks Eric.

"My father decided to take us back to Ethiopia," answers Mahamoud as he stirs some milk into his mix. "We went to an Islamic (*Is-LAH-mik*) school in Ethiopia for a couple of years before we moved to Minnesota.

"What was it like going to school in Ethiopia?"

"School was okay. We studied two languages, English and Arabic. We studied math and science. And we studied the Koran."

"What's the Koran?"

"The Koran is the Muslim holy book. We're Muslim. How about you?"

"My family is Christian. But guess what? I just moved to Minnesota a few years ago."

"Really?" asks Mahamoud. "Where are you from?"

Eric was born in Chicago, Illinois. His family moved to Minnesota in 1996 so his mother could study at the University of Minnesota.

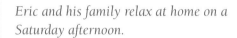

Eric and his family relax at home on a Saturday afternoon.

Getting to School
in Chicago and Ethiopia

"I'm from Chicago," answers Eric as he mixes sugar into his potatoes. "My family decided to move here so my mom could study at the University of Minnesota. We just packed up our blue car and drove here."

"What was your school like in Chicago?" asks Mahamoud.

"It was all right. I studied the same kinds of things I study in Minnesota. But there wasn't much to do at recess in Chicago. The playground was just a whole bunch of **concrete** there. My new school has lots of grass and stuff to climb on."

"We didn't have a playground at my school in Ethiopia, either. But we did get a lot of exercise."

"What do you mean?" asks Eric.

"Well, we lived one mile from school, and there weren't any sidewalks. We had to walk down a hill, cross a small river, walk along a city wall, and cross through an outdoor market. It got really muddy when it rained."

"In Chicago, I only had to walk a half-block to school!"

"Walk? You're lucky. Sometimes we had to run to school in Ethiopia."

"Why?"

"Some bullies tried to steal our pencils and paper every day because we were the new kids in the neighborhood. We had to outrun them. Now I take a school bus."

"I guess you're glad you're in Minnesota now."

"Yeah," answers Mahamoud sniffing some sweet spices for the pie. "But I miss my grandparents back in Somalia."

"I miss my family back in Chicago, too. I even miss my older cousin Michelle. She lived downstairs from me, and we used to play together. We took care of our dog, Destiny."

"Do you have anything that reminds you of Chicago?"

"I've got a Michael Jordan poster. I brought it to Minnesota from Chicago."

"Hey, I like basketball, too," says Mahamoud.

"You do?"

"I like playing basketball at the park near our apartment," Mahamoud explains. "But I don't like it when it's so cold, and I can't play outside. In Somalia, it's hot all year. I can't wait until the snow melts."

"It gets cold in Chicago, just like here in Minnesota. The wind is so strong in the winter in Chicago, we call it 'The Hawk.' When it was too cold to play outside, I used to draw at home."

"I like drawing, too!" smiles Mahamoud.

Fighting for Freedom in the United States

Eric and Mahamoud pour the sweet potato mix into the piecrust. Now it's time to bake their pies. They carry the pies up to the front of the classroom. A woman from the History Center puts their pies in the oven and tells them they will have to wait 20 minutes.

Minnesota is home to many artists. Musician Prince wore the outfit pictured above in the movie Purple Rain. Painter Alvin Carter (left) painted this mural in Minneapolis and made the drawings in this book.

"No problem," says Eric. "It's time to watch the play about Dr. Martin Luther King."

"Are you going to the play, too?" Mahamoud asks Eric.

"Of course. That's why I came to the History Center today!" answers Eric.

As they make their way up the stairs, Eric and Mahamoud pretend to slide on the railing. "Why do *you* want to watch the play about Dr. King?" asks Mahamoud, gripping the gold rail.

"Dr. King is a hero! People all around the world respect his work helping black Americans in our country. Dr. King even won the world-famous Nobel Peace Prize."

"Really?"

"Yes. But then he got shot. Some people didn't like his work."

Eric and Mahamoud reach the third floor. They join a large group of people watching the play. An actor is pretending to be Dr. King. Eric and Mahamoud learn about the time Dr. King was put in jail because he **demonstrated** for equality. The actor reads part of a letter Dr. King wrote from jail. In his letter, he shares one of the reasons he fought for equality:

> [Try] to explain to your six-year-old daughter why she can't go to the public amusement park that has just been advertised on television, and see tears

welling up in her eyes when she is told that Funtown is closed to colored children.

At the end of the play, Eric and Mahamoud hear a loud pretend shot. Dr. King has been killed. The play is over. The boys are quiet as they walk downstairs to get their pies. They don't want any more wars or murders.

Eric and Mahamoud's Future

"My family moved to Minnesota so we could be safe and have a good future. I'm glad Dr. King fought for equality," says Mahamoud.

"Me, too. Dr. King dreamed everyone should have an equal chance in our country. And when I grow up, I want to own a company and be the boss," says Eric.

"I want to be an airplane pilot," says Mahamoud.

As they near the classroom, Eric sniffs the air. "Hey, our pies smell pretty good!"

"I can't wait to try some," says Mahamoud.

"Yeah, making sweet potato pie wasn't such a bad idea after all." Then Eric and Mahamoud dive into their pies.

Today was an important day for Eric and Mahamoud. They learned about some of the contributions African Americans have made to the United States by watching the play about Dr. King and by making sweet potato pie. They also learned a lot by talking to one another.

Eric and Mahamoud learned that they have many things in common. They are both 10 years old. They are both in fourth grade. They both like basketball and drawing. They both moved to Minnesota a few years ago. But the boys also found some

Eric and Mahamoud talk to Marvin Grays, the actor who played Dr. Martin Luther King, Jr., at a Martin Luther King Day celebration at the Minnesota History Center in St. Paul.

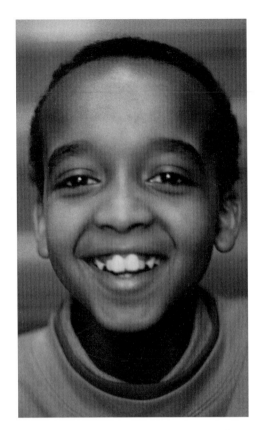

differences. Eric and Mahamoud didn't take the same journey from Africa to Minnesota. Eric's ancestors were forced to leave Africa 200 years ago. Mahamoud's family had to leave Somalia but came to Minnesota by choice just recently.

Between 1900 and 1990, the African American **population** in Minnesota grew from 5,000 to almost 100,000. Three important African American Minnesota leaders in the 1990s include

Minnesota Supreme Court Justice Alan Page, Minneapolis Mayor Sharon Sayles Belton, and St. Paul Chief of Police William Finney. It's too early to say for sure, but who knows? Maybe Eric and Mahamoud will grow up to become important leaders in Minnesota, too. One thing is certain: both boys have already made an important contribution to Minnesota history—they shared their stories with each other and with you!

Mahamoud Aden Amin would like to be an airplane pilot when he grows up.

Eric Mosley would like to own his own company when he grows up.

Glossary

abolitionist: a person who tries to end slavery

accomplish: to succeed or reach a goal

accountant: a person who keeps track of the money a company spends and earns

ancestor: a person related to you who is no longer alive

barbershop: a place where people get their hair cut

barracks: basic housing for people in the armed forces

beat: the area where a police officer works

canoe: a boat with pointed ends, originally made from trees

community: a group of people who have things in common

concrete: a hard mix of sand, water, and rock

conference: a large meeting or gathering

continent: one of the world's seven large land masses, such as North America or Africa

dairy: a place where milk and milk products are made or sold

demonstrated: expressed beliefs in a public gathering

demonstrations: gatherings where people express their beliefs

discriminated: having treated a person unfairly, often because of race

efforts: hard work, attempts, tries

encourage: to give hope and support

extended: something that is larger or longer

griot: a historian from West Africa

guarded: protected from danger

historian: a person who studies the past

horse trolley: a long car or bus powered by horses

ice rink: a flat, frozen surface used for ice skating

industry: a group of businesses that make similar goods

inspired: encouraged to take action

interpreter: a person who explains what people are saying in different languages

interview: to get information from a person by asking a set of questions

invention: a new discovery or device

kerosene: a special thin oil used for heating and lighting

lumber: logs or trees that are cut into boards for building

lynching: the murder of a person by a group of people

mills: buildings with machines that make products such as lumber or flour

minister: a person who leads a church

neighborhood: a place where people live near one another

noose: a long rope with a round loop at one end, used for lynchings or hangings

pelts: stretched, cleaned animal skins with the fur still on

piecrust: the bottom and top part of a pie, made from flour

pinafore: an apron worn over a dress, to keep it clean

politics: the way people work together to run the government

population: the whole number of people living in an area

pushcart: a toy car with no engine, go-cart

raft: a simple, flat boat made from wood

refereed: was in charge of a sports game

refugee: a person who has to leave his/her country to find safety

road slip: a square metal tool used to clear roads

routes: paths, roads

scholarship: money given to a student for education

segregate: to separate one group from another group

slave: a person who is owned by another person and is not free

slavery: a system in which a certain group of people have no freedom

stagecoach: a four-wheeled vehicle powered by horses

steamboat: a large boat powered by steam and used on rivers

streetcar: a long car or bus powered by electricity:

sweet potato: a starchy, orange vegetable

trade goods: things people buy and sell

traditional: handed down over time as a special thing or custom

treaty: an agreement between two or more nations

typewriter: a hand-operated machine with keys that prints letters and numbers

veterans: people who served in the armed forces:

victories: wins

voyageurs: men hired to transport trade goods and pelts in canoes

waterproof: able to keep dry in the rain

Selected Bibliography

	Abbreviations
MHS	Minnesota Historical Society, St. Paul
MM-G	Mary Murphy-Gnatz
OHC	Oral History Collections

Storytelling and History

Asante, Molefi K. *African American History: A Journey of Liberation*. Maywood, N.J.: Peoples Publishing Group, Inc., 1995.

_____, and Mark T. Mattson. *The Historical and Cultural Atlas of African Americans*. New York: Macmillan, 1991.

Davidson, Basil. *Africa in History: Themes and Outlines*. Rev. and expanded ed. New York: Collier Books, 1991.

_____. *African Civilization Revisited: From Antiquity to Modern Times*. Trenton, N.J.: Africa World Press, 1991.

Gilman, Rhoda R. *The Story of Minnesota's Past*. 1989. Reprint, St. Paul: MHS Press, 1991.

Lawrence, Harold. "African Explorers in the New World." *The Crisis* (National Association for the Advancement of Colored People), June–July 1962, p. 321–32.

Niane, Djibril Tamsir. *Sundiata: An Epic of Old Mali*. Translated by G. D. Pickett. London: Longmans, 1965.

Spangler, Earl. *The Negro in Minnesota*. Minneapolis: T. S. Denison, 1961.

Taylor, David V. "The Blacks." In *They Chose Minnesota: A Survey of the State's Ethnic Groups*, ed. June Drenning Holmquist, p. 73–91. St. Paul: MHS Press, 1981.

_____, comp. *Blacks in Minnesota: A Preliminary Guide to Historical Sources*. St. Paul: MHS, 1976.

Van Sertima, Ivan. *They Came before Columbus*. New York: Random House, 1976.

Meet George Bonga

Bonga, George. "The Letters of George Bonga." *Journal of Negro History* 12 (January 1927): 41–54.

Gilman, Carolyn. *Where Two Worlds Meet: The Great Lakes Fur Trade*. Museum Exhibit Series, no. 2. St. Paul: MHS, 1982.

Nute, Grace Lee. *The Voyageur*. 1931. Reprint, St. Paul: MHS Press, 1987.

Porter, Kenneth W. "Negroes and the Fur Trade." *Minnesota History* (MHS) 15 (December 1934): 421–33.

Meet William Grey and John Hickman

Douglass, Frederick. *Autobiographies*. The Library of America, 68. New York: Library of America, 1994.

"Finch, Van Slyck, McConville Auditor Receives Much Praise." *Northwestern Bulletin* (St. Paul and Minneapolis), April 26, 1924, p. 1, 4.

Green, William D. "Minnesota's Long Road to Black Suffrage, 1849–1868." *Minnesota History* 56 (summer 1998): 68–84.

Grey, Emily O. Goodridge. "The Black Community in Territorial St. Anthony: A Memoir." Ed. Patricia C. Harpole. *Minnesota History* 49 (summer 1984): 42–53.

Hickman, John, Sr. "Reminiscences of Earlier St. Paul." *Northwestern Bulletin*, May 5, 1923, p. 1, 4.

Meet Mattie McIntosh

Frank, Melvin Lynn. "In North Minneapolis: Sawmill City Boyhood." *Minnesota History* 47 (winter 1980): 141–53.

History of the Police and Fire Departments of the Twin Cities: Their Origin in Early Village Days and Progress to 1900. Minneapolis: American Land & Title Register Association, 1899.

"N.A.A.C.: The National Afro–American Council." *The Appeal* (St. Paul and Minneapolis), July 19, 1902, p. 1–2.

Taylor, David V. "John Quincy Adams: St. Paul Editor and Black Leader." *Minnesota History* 43 (winter 1973): 282–96.

Webster, Polletta Vera Leonard. Interview by David V. Taylor. July 8, 1974. Minnesota Black History Project, OHC, MHS Collections.

Meet Nellie Stone Johnson

"Duluth Mob Hangs 3 Negroes to Avenge Young Girl." *Minneapolis Morning Tribune*, June 16, 1920, p. 1–2.

Fedo, Michael. *The Lynchings in Duluth*. Foreword by William D. Green. 1979. Reprint, St. Paul: MHS Press, Borealis Books, 2000.

Johnson, Nellie Stone. Interview by MM-G. July 28, 1998. OHC, MHS.

_____. Interview by David V. Taylor. July 15, 1975. Minnesota Black History Project, OHC, MHS Collections.

Roberts, Norene. "A Woman's Place in Minnesota" issue of *Roots* (MHS), vol. 9, no. 2 (winter 1981): 24–27.

Meet James Griffin

Griffin, James S. *Blacks in the St. Paul Police and Fire Departments, 1885–1976*. St. Paul: E & J Inc., 1978.

_____. Interview by MM-G. July 30, 1998. OHC, MHS.

_____. James S. Griffin Papers. MHS Collections.

Parks, Gordon. *A Choice of Weapons*. 1966. Reprint, St. Paul: MHS Press, Borealis Books, 1986.

Meet David Taylor

Fairbanks, Evelyn. *The Days of Rondo*. St. Paul: MHS Press, 1990.

Taylor, David V. "The Black Community in the Twin Cities." In "Black Minnesotans" issue of *Roots*, vol. 17, no. 1 (fall 1988): 3–22.

_____. "Growing up in St. Paul: Looking Back at the Black Community." Parts I (with Eula T. Murphy) and II. *Ramsey County History* (Ramsey County [Minn.] Historical Society), vol. 27 (winter 1992–93): 12–15; vol. 28 (spring 1993): 19–23.

_____. Interview by MM-G. August 13, 1998. OHC, MHS.

Meet Eric Mosley and Mahamoud Aden Amin

Awil, Aden Amin, and family. Interview by MM-G. August 14, 1998. OHC, MHS.

Fox, Mary Virginia. _Somalia_. Enchantment of the World series. New York: Children's Press, 1996.

King, Martin Luther, Jr. _Letter from the Birmingham Jail_. San Francisco: Harper San Francisco, 1994.

Mosley, Eric, and Yvette Pye. Interview by MM-G. August 25, 1998. OHC, MHS.

United States. Bureau of the Census. _1990 Census of Population and Housing: Summary Population and Housing Characteristics: Minnesota_. Washington, D.C.: U.S. Department of Commerce, Economics and Statistics Administration, Bureau of the Census, 1991.

Index